TARGET &
APPROACH TONES

Shaping Bebop Lines

by Joe Riposo

Published by
JAMEY AEBERSOLD JAZZ®
P.O. Box 1244
New Albany, IN 47151-1244
www.jazzbooks.com
ISBN 978-1-56224-263-3

Cover Design
JASON A. LINDSEY

FOREWORD

Most players learn scales and practice using them over chord changes but still cannot produce a musical sentence. Their improvised melodic line played over chord changes does not connect the chords together. The line sounds like it is played over each individual chord without the relationship of the parent scale. Even if the right scale notes are played on the individual chords, the improvised line fails to make musical sense. The line does not have the maturity of a musical phrase or line direction

A musical improved line must contain the following elements:

1. Target Tones, Peak & Focus Tones
2. Hinge Tones
3. Points of Resolution
4. Approach Tones
5. Tension and Release Tones
6. Most important of all an improvised melodic line must have Shape and Forward Motion.

The goal of this book is to demonstrate this concept and provide instruction as to how one can develop the skill of playing phrases which include the elements of jazz phasing.

No one can create the improvised melodic line for you. One can only provide you with the concepts and guide your practice from which you will learn to hear and feel the improvised melodic line. You are the only one who can create the line in your mind and learn to play what you hear. Before you get to this desired point in your musical experience, you are encouraged to make musical decisions that will add this concept to your playing.

You can accomplish this by practicing chord changes of many standard jazz tunes using different approach tones leading to different target tones. This practice will allow you to become more fluent in playing an improvised melodic line that contains the elements of a mature improvised line.

INTRODUCTION

A **target tone** is a specific note in a chord which gives the melodic line focus and direction. Each note in a scale gives a melodic line different color. Some notes in a scale played over a chord sound better than others. For example: the 3rd note of a scale gives the scale tonality and focus. This note makes the scale sound major or minor. The 7th note of a scale is referred to as a hinge tone. It allows one to hinge chords together. The 7th note of a scale allows one to navigate from one chord to another. At this stage of your musical experience the best two notes to use as target tones would be the 3rd and 7th notes of a scale. This is not to say that all the other notes in a scale are not important or not good notes to use as target tones. The remaining scale tones provide different colors to the solo line. The only note one should avoid would be the 4th note of a major and dominant scale. This note is referred to as an avoidance tone. One can make this note usable by raising it one half step. (#4)

Approach tones are notes used to arrive at the target tones. These tones are sometimes a scale tone away from the target tone and sometimes one half step away from the target tone. One can expand the approach tones to include a part of a scale using the target tone as the "peak" tone to aim for. Approach tones lead to the target notes in the new chord. This is what gives the improvised line direction and forward motion. One may have many target tones in a line that can be approached in different ways.

HOW TO USE THIS BOOK

The first few pages of this book will provide you with the theory needed to begin to understand why target and approach tones are so important in the improvised melodic line.

There are three basic levels involved in the learning process:

- Developing a *knowledge* of --------------- (Facts)
- Developing an *understanding* of ---------- (Conceptualization)
- Most important of all, *application* of ----- (Using what you learned)

This book is divided into three sections. In the first section we will discuss some basic jazz theory that will help you to accumulate knowledge. In the second section you will develop your understanding of the knowledge obtained. This is when you will conceptualize the knowledge. In the last section of the book you will be provided the opportunity to apply your knowledge. Needless to say, this is the most important part of the learning sequence. Here is where you practice to perfect what has been learned in the previous sections of the book.

This is the format used in this book to share with you the experience of learning how and why you need to include the target and approach tones in your improvised melodic line.

The jazz theory presented in this book will help you to develop that phase of learning called *developing knowledge of.* These are the facts one needs to know at the beginning stage of learning to use target and approach tones. Do not get frustrated at this point because you will not yet be expected to use the knowledge. Remember the basic levels of learning.

You will also be provided with many examples of how you can use the jazz theory presented. By playing these examples and remembering the theory surrounding the manufacturing of the examples, you will begin to build the understanding of the theory.

Now comes the most important part of the book. We will call this part of the learning process the application of the knowledge of which you have developed an understanding. Once again the important three words are: Knowledge, Understanding and Application.

For the application of knowledge we will use the chord changes from the song **"JO ANN"** taken from one of my earlier published books Jazz Improvisation **"A Whole-Brain Approach."** These chord changes will allow you to learn a variety of target and approach tones.

In the first sixteen measures of the tune "JoAnn," all the target and approach tones are written to provide an example demonstrating how they can be used. The next sixteen measures are left blank so you can play your own target and approach tones. This now becomes the application of the concept learned. The first sixteen measures is a part of the teaching process and your work on the last sixteen measures now become the learning process.

Keep in mind the most important part of this process is the application. You should practice using this teaching/learning sequence with every tune you would like to learn. The more you use approach tones and target tones the faster you will be able to automatically apply this concept to your improvised line. I strongly suggest you use the Jamey Aebersold Play-A-Long recordings and use your newly developed improvisational skill of playing with target and approach tones. Jamey Aebersold provides you with your own private rhythm section to practice with. It is important to hear your improvised line over chord changes played by a rhythm section. One needs to develop that sound factory we all have in our brain. The more you hear your improvised line over standard jazz chord changes the faster you will experience a transfer of knowledge to other jazz tunes.

Enjoy and have fun. I thank you for allowing me to share with you this musical experience.

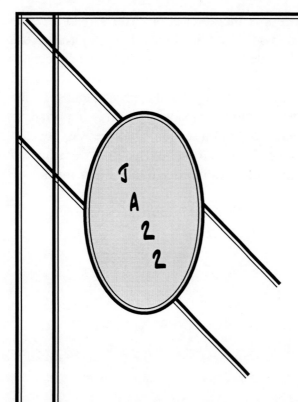

DEVELOPING KNOWLEDGE

"JAZZ THEORY"

NOTES & COMMENTS

THEORY: TARGET TONES
MAJOR SCALE

If you played the tonic chord on each note of a Major scale you will find that some notes sound better than others in terms of color. Use your ear to discover which notes sound colorful and which notes sound harsh. By playing the chord on each scale tone you will hear how some notes complement the chord's color while others clash.

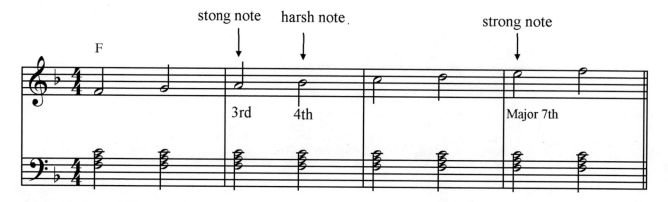

The 3rd of the scale is the strongest tone in terms of providing the most color to the melodic line. The 7th is the next most important tone. Both the 3rd and 7th notes of the scale are great target tones to aim for in your improvised line.

A harsh dissonant sound is produced when the chord is played on the 4th note of the scale. You should not stop on this note or give it any importance in your improvised line. This note should not be used as a target tone. It can only be used and sound good if you raise the pitch one half step. It now becomes the #4 that is used frequently in the jazz line.

All the other notes in a major scale are usable and complement the chord with different tone colors. Some notes will give the chord tension like the 2nd and the #4 while others give the chord release and resolution like the 3rd, 6th and 1st. The 5th note of the scale is an empty sounding note. It provides little color to the melodic line.

Listed below is a ranking of notes in order of suggested importance from top to bottom in a major scale.

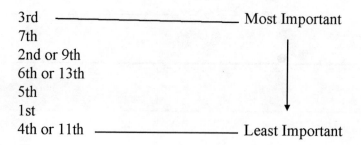

THEORY: APPROACH TONES
NON-CHORDAL TONES

Approach tones can be scale or non-chordal tones. Non-chordal tones are notes that do not appear in a chord, chord extension or scale. The # 2 and # 4 of a major and dominant scale are called non-chordal tones

When the #2 or #4 are used as approach tones they must resolve upward to a chord tone. These non-chordal tones can add additional color to the existing row of notes used in developing a melodic line.

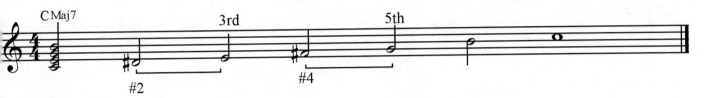

Notice in the example above the #2 resolved up to the 3rd of the chord (E) and the #4 resolved up to the 5th of the chord (G).

Here is an example of how the #2 can be used as an approach tone.

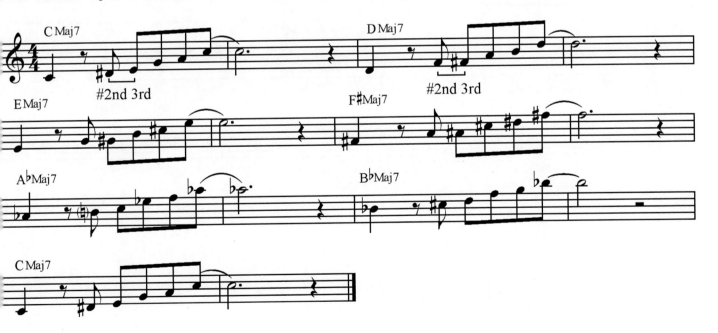

Play this example and listen how the #2 gives the line color and direction.

Here is another example of how non-chordal tones can be used as approach tones. Play this example and listen to how the approach tones (non- chordal tones) lead your ear to hear the resolution to the chord tone. By analyzing this example you will build your understanding of how and why target and approach tones are so essential to shapethe improvised melodic line.

Use your ear and play this example in all keys. Only the first half is written so you can use your ear to complete the example. Do not write the notation in the blank measures. Remember, it is all about developing your ear to hear the target and approach tones.

Playing this exercise in all keys will help to develop your ear to hear how non-chordal tones work.

Example 1. Use of (#2 and #4)

ere is another example of how non-chordal tones can be used as approach tones. Play the example and listen
  how the approach tones (non-chordal tones) lead your ear to hear the resolution to the chord tone. By
analyzing these examples you will build your understanding of why target and approach tones are so essential
  shape the improvised melodic line.

his example sounds more like an improvised jazz line. Examine this example to discover what contributes to the
und of the line.To develop your ear to hear these non-chordal tones play this example in all keys. Look at how
e non-chordal notes are used to connect the line together. This is the continuity that should be present in a jazz
ne.

his next example still only uses the #2 and #4 to create a jazz line. You should use your ear and create
ur own line using the #2 and #4

Example 2. Use of (#2 and #4)

THEORY: TARGET TONES

DORIAN SCALE

Unlike the Major scale, all the notes in a Dorian scale sound good. Any note in the Dorian scale can be used as a target tone. Once again you need to listen for the notes that sound better than others. The 3rd and 7th note of the scale are still the best notes to use. There is one note in this scale that is the most important note and that is the 6th. The reason the 6th is the most important note in the Dorian scale is because it is the note that gives this scale the unique Dorian sound .

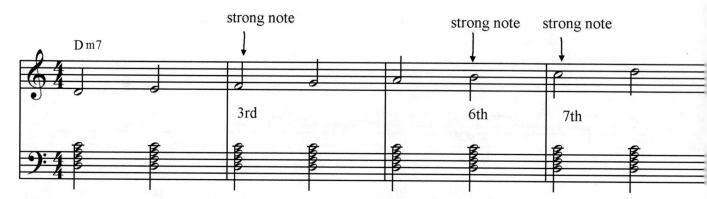

Play the example above and listen how the color changes with each note. Remember all the notes in the Dorian scale are great notes to use as target tones. Listen how strong the 6th, 3rd and 7th notes sound.

To develop your ear to hear the quality of each note in the Dorian scale, explore by aiming and stopping on a different note and listen to how it sounds. (See the example below.)

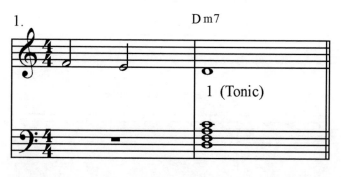

In this example we selected to use the 1st note of the scale as the target tone. Listen how empty this tone sounds with the chord relationship.

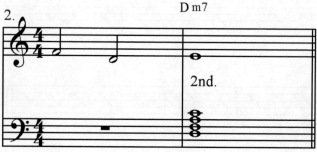

In this example we selected the 2nd note of the scale as our target tone. Listen to the different tone qualities produced. This note has a bright quality with the chord relationship.

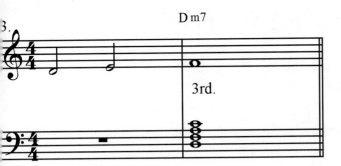

3.

D m7

3rd.

In this example we selected the 3rd as our target tone. Listen to the rich tone quality it produces. It is the focus tone of the chord which makes the chord sound restful.

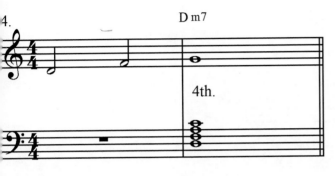

4.

D m7

4th.

Here we used the 4th as our target tone. Unlike in the Major scale the 4th in the Dorian scale is a good note to use. It is a bright sound and has some friction which gives it motion.

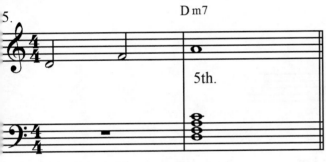

5.

D m7

5th.

This example uses the 5th of the scale as the target tone. It is empty in sound and does not add much color to the chord.

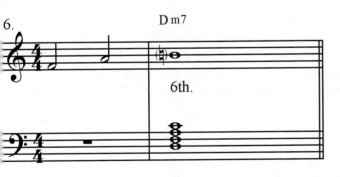

6.

D m7

6th.

The 6th is one of the best notes in a Dorian scale to use as a target tone. This is the note that makes the scale sound Dorian. (A valuable note)

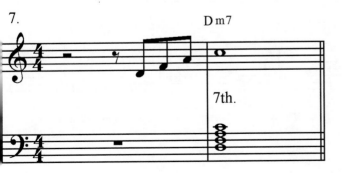

7.

D m7

7th.

The 7th as a target tone makes the line sound like it has to resolve. It creates forward motion.

THEORY: LINE DIRECTION

Building the forward motion in the solo line

The improvised line must have shape and direction. An improvised line needs to be thought of as a musical sentence. To shape the direction of a phrase it needs to contain forward motion.

Two elements need to be considered which provide forward motion.

- Aim for one of the strong notes of the new chord.
- End the phrase over the bar line on the new chord.

Example 1.

Example 2.

Notice that the last note of the phrase in example 1 is the 3rd of the new chord (Cm7) and the last note of the phrase in example 2 is the 7th of the new chord. These two musical sentences extend over the bar line into the new harmonic structure which gives the phrase its forward motion.

Practice creating an improvised line on the following chord progressions. Select the 3rd or 7th of the new chord to aim for as the target tone. Example 3 is the mental picture of the concept you should develop. Example 4 demonstrates how we get to the target tones using approach tones.

Example 3.

Example 4.

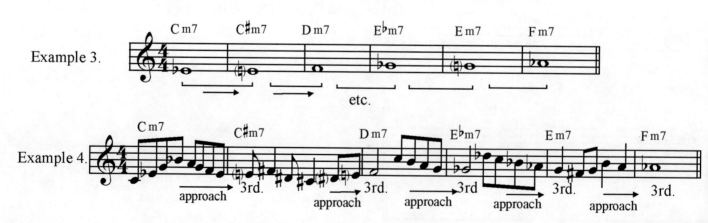

THEORY: TARGET TONES

DOMINANT SCALE

If you played a Dominant scale and played the V7 chord on each tone, you will find that some notes sound better than others. Use your ear to discover which notes sound colorful and which notes sound harsh. By playing the chord on each scale tone you will hear how some notes complement the chord's color while others clash. The Dominant scale is much like the Major scale in that the 4th is not a good note to stop on.

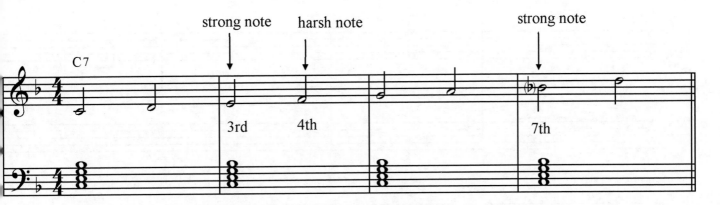

The 3rd of the Dominant scale is the strongest tone in terms of providing the most color to the melodic line. The 7th is the next most important tone.

A harsh dissonant sound is produced when the chord is played on the 4th note of the scale. You should not stop on this note or give it any importance in your improvised line. This note should not be used as a target tone. It can only be used and sound good if you raise the pitch one half step. It now becomes a #4 that is played frequentlyin a jazz line.

All the other notes in a Dominant scale are usable and complement the chord with different tone colors. Some notes will give the chord tension like the 2nd and the #4 while others give the chord release and resolution like the 3rd, 6th and 1st. The 5th note of the scale is usable but produces an empty sound and offers little color to the melodic line.

Listed below is a ranking of notes in order of suggested importance from top to bottom in a Dominant scale.

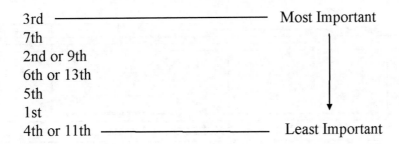

As in the Major scale, not all the notes in a Dominant scale sound good. Some notes can be used as a target tone while other notes should not be used. Once again you need to listen for the notes that sound better than others. The 3rd and 7th note of the Dominant scale are still the best notes to use.

Play the example below and listen to how the color changes with each note played. We will start on the 3rd of the chord and aim for the 7th of the chord or scale. This example will help you to hear the importance of the use of the 3rd and 7th in an improvised line.

9

Make up your own line over the same chord progression using the 3th and 7th of each chord.

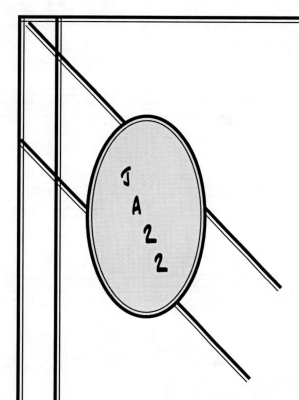

DEVELOPING AN UNDERSTANDING

"CONCEPTUALIZATION"

NOTES & COMMENTS

UNDERSTANDING TARGET TONES

To begin to develop an understanding of the use of target tones let us take the most often used jazz progression. In the middle section of a jazz tune called the bridge, you will at times see a V7 chord resolving to another V7 chord called the cycle of 4ths or sometimes called cycle of 5ths.

We need to think in terms of a line that is played through chord changes and not up and down on a chord. To demonstrate this concept play the 3rds and 7ths of the chords in the progression below:

Notice when you play the 3rd and 7th on this chord progression it produces a chromatic scale. This choice of notes help to navigate through each chord in this standard jazz progression.

With this concept in mind, if we added approach tones from the chord scales you will develop a melodic line. The 3rds will now become the target tones and the connecting tone, the 7ths, will become the approach tone .

A player must become aware of certain pitches within a chord or scale which seems to be harmonically "more important" than others. For example the 3rd note of a Dominant chord (called the focus tone) conveys its quality and the 7th of a Dominant chord is used as a "hinge" tone which allows the player to resolve to the next chord. The use of the hinge tone gives the improvised line direction and it helps to create motion which is frequently missing in the beginner's solo line. Focus tones are great notes to aim for in a melodic line. The use of hinge tone begin to shape the approach tone phrase.

Play the example below and listen to how the notes function with the chords. Notice how the 7th resolves to the 3rd of the new chord.

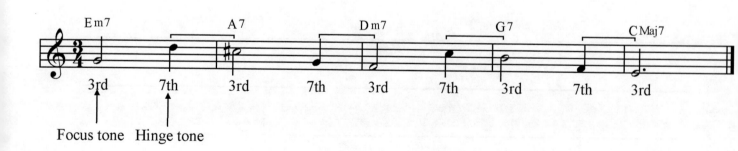

UNDERSTANDING TARGET TONES

The 3rd of the scale is the strongest tone in terms of providing the most color for the melodic line. The 7th is the next most important tone of a chord that resolves to the next chord. The hinge tone is a great note to use as an approach tone. Notice the line direction created with the use of the 7th. (Hinge tone)

Once again play the 3rds and 7ths as written on the progression above and listen how these notes function with the chords. You can now hear line direction in the phrase. The 3rd focuses the chord's quality and the 7th (the hinge tone) resolves to the next chord.

As you can see in the example above, we have created a melodic line by adding only a few scale notes in between the target and approach tones.

In the next example we have articulated the ii7 chord to approach the target tone. Notice the 7th of the chord resolves to the 3rd of the new chord, which makes an interesting line.

Notice the direction and forward motion the line takes on by aiming for the 3rd of the new chord. This is the kind of a line you would hear in many jazz solos.

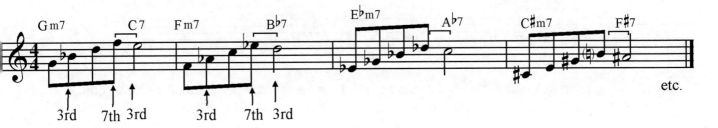

LINE DIRECTION

(Building an understanding of line direction)

More theory to help build a better understanding of why approach and target tones are needed in the improvised melodic line. The 7th becomes a desirable note to use as an approach tone because it resolves to the 3rd of the new chord.

The concept here is using the 3rd as the target tone and the 7th as the approach tone. As stated earlier these tone provide the improvised solo line direction. By articulating the chord notes aiming for the 3rd of the new chord v now begin to hear a melodic line emerging.

Aiming toward the target tone the 3rd of the new chord creats in the listener's ear a desire to hear the resolution The ear wants to hear the 7th of the chord (Hinge tone) resolve to the 3rd of the new chord. (Target tone)

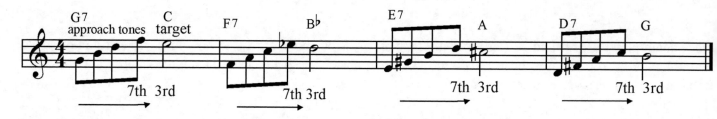

Important concept to remember: *A phrase should end on a note in the resolving chord.* The best target tone to use for this is the 3rd of the new chord thus encompassing two harmonic structures. This technique creates direction in the solo line.

Let us insert the ii minor chord in front of the V7 chord. Listen how it increases the flow of the line. Once again this is because the ear wants to hear the 7th resolve to the 3rd of the new chord.

Notice how the approach tones lead your ear to want to hear the target tones. (3rd of the new chord.)

The next examples demonstrate the concept discussed on the previous pages over a typical jazz chord progression. Notice the line direction and how fluent the line sounds. The line takes on a continuous flow through to the end of the exercise. This is because of the 7th resolves to the 3rd of each chord. The line sounds connected, which creates the *forward motion* and pulls your ear to the resolution.

The brackets indicate the approach tones leading to the 3rd.

This is an other example of how the 7th is used as an approach tone and the 3rd as a target tone.

In this next example the b9th is added to the approach tones. Listen how this tone adds motion and direction to the line. It makes the line sound smoother by taking the corners off the progression. This line definitely has the shape that makes it sound interesting to the ear.

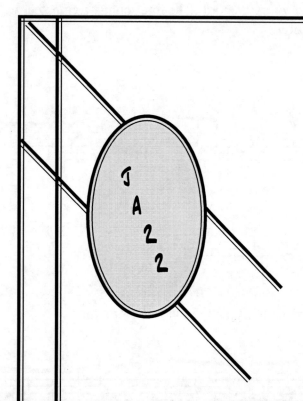

APPLICATION

"USING WHAT HAS BEEN LEARNED"

NOTES & COMMENTS

APPLICATION OF KNOWLEDGE
"USING WHAT HAS BEEN LEARNED"

You have now completed two phases of the learning process: developing knowledge of (Jazz Theory) and developing an understanding of (Conceptualization). Up to this point you have acquired knowledge of jazz theory, which is the first cell of the learning phase. It is during this phase of learning you have accumulated a lot of facts that helped you to enter the second phase of learning.

During the second phase of learning you have developed an understanding of the knowledge obtained. At this point you began to put facts together and conceptualized the knowledge accumulated. You now are putting the parts of the puzzle together to see the big picture of how jazz theory works and is used. This is an important part of the process because if you do not develop this understanding you will not convert knowledge into meaningful knowledge, usable knowledge.

Music (Jazz Improvisation) is a language and must be learned as such. Target tones are much like nouns in the English language and Approach tones are like verbs and descriptive adjectives.

The target tone (noun) is the main subject of the improvised line. The approach tones (adjectives, verbs, etc.) describe the target tones (nouns). These approach tones lead to the target tone and give meaning to that note (noun). The difference between the English language and the language of music is in the English language a word has a fixed meaning. One word standing alone has meaning such as: fire, love, pain, etc. You know immediately what the word means. In the language of music a note does not have a fixed meaning. A note only takes on meaning when it is associated with other notes. This is why approach tones are extremely important in the improvised line. The target tone only takes on meaning when it is associated with approach tones.

We do not learn by practicing but, contrary to what some people believe, we practice to perfect what we have learned. If you have successfully completed the first two phases of learning you are ready to enter the third phase. You now need to practice to perfect what you have learned in phases one and two. This is turning knowledge into usable, meaningful knowledge. Now you will experience application of knowledge that is using what has been learned.

Earlier we listed the three basic levels involved in the learning process.

Developing a knowledge of -----------------------(Fact)
Developing an understanding of ------------------ (Conceptualization)
Application of ------------------------------------- (Using what has been learned)

The third and last phase of this book will allow you to apply what you have learned. In this section of the book you will be exposed to a model that should be used to learn to play any tune. Practice this sequence with all the Jamey Aebersold Play-A-Long recordings. These Play-A-Long recordings are a great resource that is available to you. Jamey Aebersold has provided you with your own private rhythm section so you can practice to perfect what you have learned. The more you play the easier it becomes and the faster you will learn to use this concept of playing. If you learn tunes using this method you will find that you will develop a deep understanding of the jazz theory of the tune and enter what I call a harmonic environment. You need to get inside the tune and develop a feel for what you are playing.

You will find that if you use this method of learning tunes you will not forget them even after not playing them for a couple of years. This is because you have not only learned the tune but the language of the tune (Jazz Theory). You will also find that this understanding and application of jazz theory will contribute to the transfer of knowledge from one tune to another. Once again with this method you will learn tunes faster by ear.

3rds AS TARGET TONES

This section of the book allows you to apply the knowledge and understanding of the knowledge you have obtained in the first part of this book. You will be practicing to perfect what you have learned. The first sixteen measures of the tune have all the target tones written providing the example of how these tones can be used. This is the teaching part of the process. Playing the next sixteen measures using your ear to hear the target tones is the application or learning part of the exercise.

We will start your practice experience using the simplest target tones and gradually building your experience to include approach tones.

Let us start with using only the 3rds of all the chords as our target tones. Remember this is the tone that allows the chord to focus its tonality.

Play the first sixteen measures as written and play the next sixteen measures in the same fashion using your ear to hear the 3rds of each chord.

JOANN

by Joe Riposo

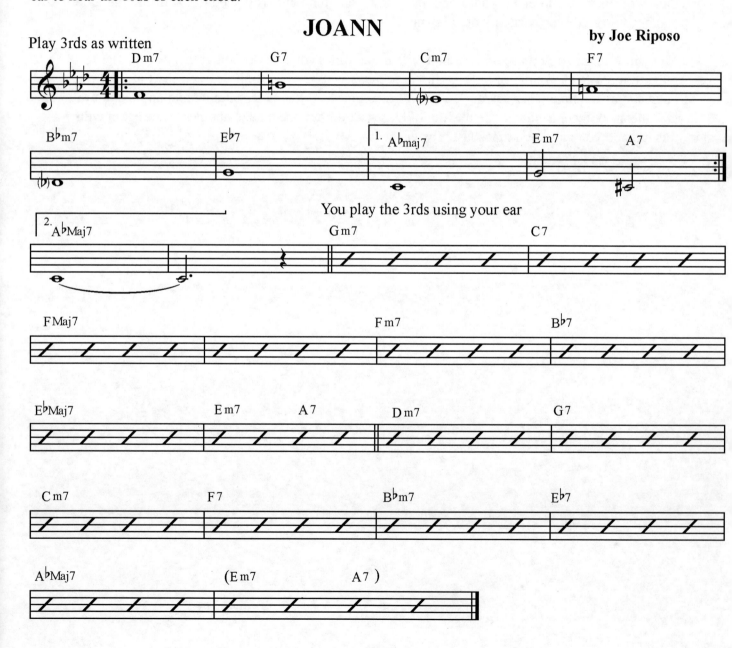

7ths AS TARGET TONES

Now that you have developed your ear to hear the 3rds of major, minor and dominant chords as target tones let us move on to the 7th of the chord as target tones. Notice the different quality of sound produced by the 7th of the chord. This note give us a different tone color with which to work.

This is the note that allows one to hinge one chord to another. Make sure that you play the major 7th when you come to the Major 7th chords. (AbMaj.7, FMaj.7 and EbMaj.7) You should always use the 7th note of the scale as the target tone.

JOANN

by Joe Riposo

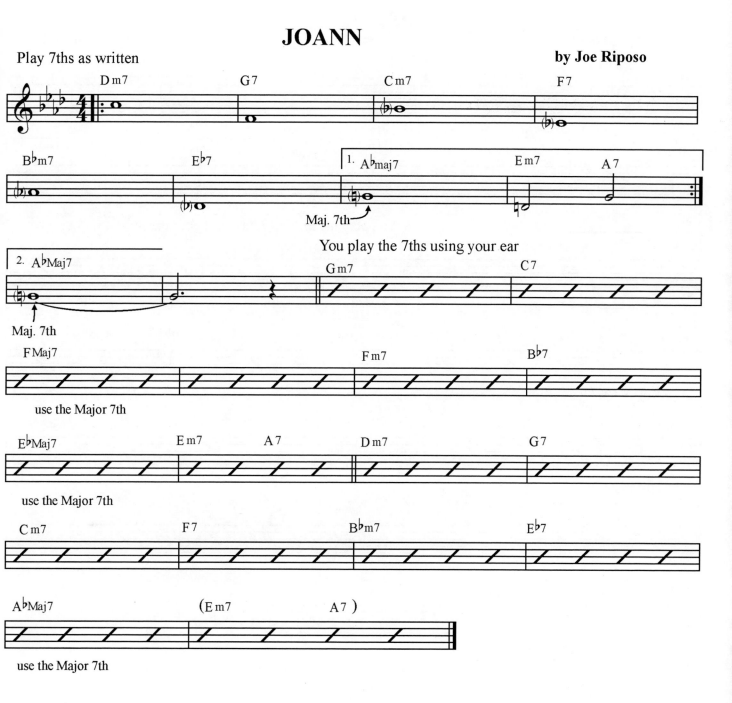

22

SCALE STEP APPROACH

The next logical step in this sequence of learning the concept of using target and approach tones is the use of both the 3rds and 7ths of chords. In this example you can see how the 7th of the chord is used as an approach tone resolving to the 3rd of the new chord as the target tone. Remember the 3rd focuses the tonality of the chord while the 7ths of a chord helps us to hinge chords together. Harmonically the 7th allows a melodic line to begin to take on shape.

Notice you are now starting to hear a melodic line with a definite shape, line direction and forward motion. The 7th allows you to comfortably move to the next chord.

JOANN

by Joe Riposo

1/2 STEP APPROACH

Once again let us go back to using the 3rd as our target tone. One can approach the target tone in this case the 3rd of the chord from a 1/2 step below. This will give the harmonic structure definition. Notice that even with using only one approach tone leading to the target tone the line begins to take on forward motion and line direction.

JOANN

by Joe Riposo

SCALE STEP APPROACH

You can also approach the target tone from one scale step above. Once again listen how the 3rd provides chord focus. With the 3rd of the chord as our target tone you can hear if the chord sounds Major, Minor or Dominant.

It is all about developing your ear to hear these approach and target tones. Remember, you are now practicing to perfect what you have learned when we discussed all the jazz theory in the first part of this book.

JOANN

by Joe Riposo

SCALE LINE TO THE 3RD

We are now ready to include a scale line aiming for the 3rd of each chord as our target tone. In this example we will use the first three note of the scale as our approach tones and aim for the 3rd of the chord as our target tone.

You will now hear the beginning of a melodic line taking shape with forward motion. Make sure you play the first three notes of a Dorian scale on minor chords (ii), Dominant scale on V7 chords and a Major scale on Major 7 chords.

JOANN

by Joe Riposo

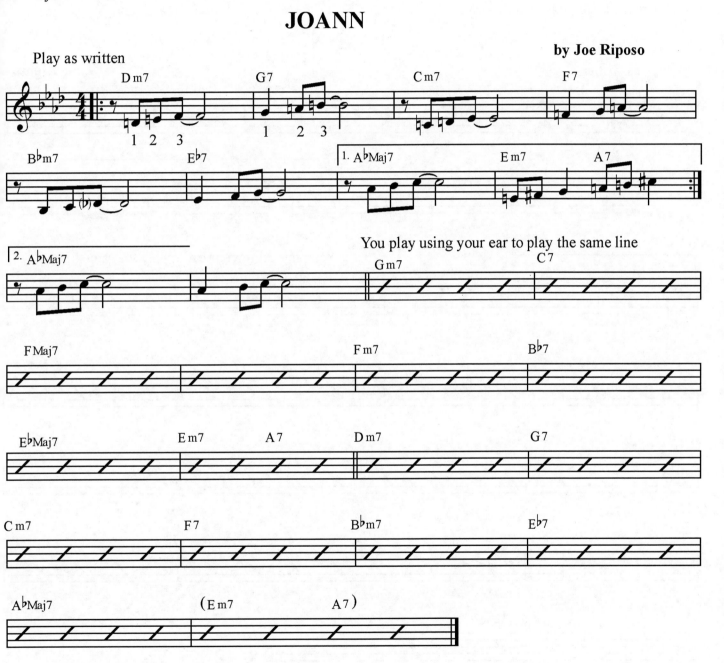

26

SCALE LINE TO THE 5TH

In this exercise let us start on the 3rd of the chord and aim for the 5th as our target tone. The 5th is not always the best note to aim for but because of the scale line used and by starting on the 3rd of the chord the line will make musical sense.

Because of the chord progression this melodic line now extends over the bar line and encompasses two chords. This gives the line a mature sound.

The 5th is the target tone, and the scale line leading to the 5th now becomes our approach tones.

JOANN

by Joe Riposo

27

SCALE LINE TO THE 7TH

In this exercise let us start on the 5th of the chord and aim for the 7th. The 7th of the scale or chord is a great note to use as a target tone. Notice the strong color quality the 7th provides to the melodic line.

Once again listen to the melodic line as it extends over the bar line and encompasses two chords. Because of the note choices, our line is now taking on more direction and forward motion.

JOANN

by Joe Riposo

28

TWO NOTE APPROACH TO THE 3RD

In this exercise we will approach the target tone, the 3rd, with three notes. We will use a scale step above the target tone and 1/2 step from below the target tone. This will provide a strong approach to the 3rd (focus tone) of the chord and give the line more direction.

The 3rd of the chord is still a great note to aim for in developing a melodic line. You should now begin to hear a stronger melodic line developing.

JOANN

by Joe Riposo

29

THREE NOTE APPROACH TO THE 3RD

Still keeping the 3rd of the chord as our target tone, we will approach it with three notes. We will use a scale step above and sometimes 1/2 step from below. This will provide a strong approach to the 3rd (focus tone) of the chord and give the line more direction. Listen to the variety of ways you can approach target tones.

The 3rd of the chord is still a great note to aim for in developing a melodic line. You should now begin to hear a stronger melodic line developing.

JOANN

by Joe Riposo

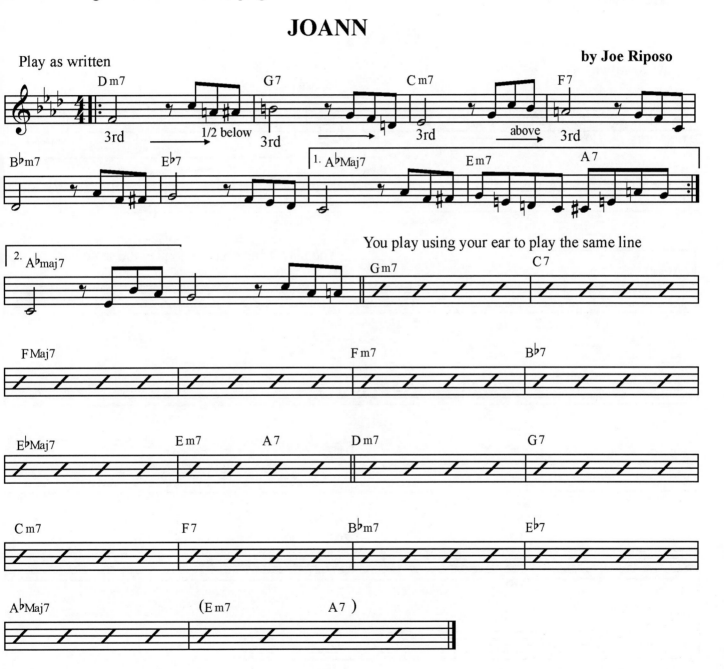

THREE NOTE APPROACH TO THE 7TH

In this exercise the 7th becomes our target tone. Still using a three-note approach, we will at times approach the target tone from a scale step above and at times from 1/2 step below. This should give the melodic line much-needed variety. The line now should be more interesting to listen to.

This three note approach makes a very strong melodic line. Listen to the line direction and forward motion we have created.

JOANN

Play as written

by Joe Riposo

31

TREBLE CLEF INSTRUMENTS:
Piano, Flute, Guitar, Violin, etc.

JOANN SOLO
#1

This is a transcribed improvised solo demonstrating the concept explained in this book. We have basically used 3rds and 7ths as target tones. At times we used 9ths and a Major 7th. Play the solo and listen and feel how the approach tones lead to the target tones.

Analyze this solo to discover how the note choices that make up the approach tones create the line direction and give the phrases forward motion.

by Joe Riposo

JOANN SOLO
#1

This is a transcribed improvised solo demonstrating the concept explained in this book. We have basically used 3rds and 7ths as target tones. At times we used 9ths and a Major 7th. Play the solo and listen and feel how the approach tones lead to the target tones.

Analyze this solo to discover how the note choices that make up the approach tones create the line direction and give the phrases forward motion.

by Joe Riposo

JOANN SOLO
#1

This is a transcribed improvised solo demonstrating the concept explained in this book. We have basically used 3rds and 7ths as target tones. At times we used 9ths and a Major 7th. Play the solo and listen and feel how the approach tones lead to the target tones.

Analyze this solo to discover how the note choices that make up the approach tones create the line direction and give the phrases forward motion.

by Joe Riposo

JOANN SOLO
#1

This is a transcribed improvised solo demonstrating the concept explained in this book. We have basically used 3rds and 7ths as target tones. At times we used 9ths and a Major 7th. As you play the solo listen and feel how the approach tones lead to the target tones.

Analyze this solo to discover how the note choices that make up the approach tones create the line direction and give the phrases forward motion.

by Joe Riposo

JOANN SOLO
#2

This is another transcribed improvised solo on the chord changes of the tune "JoAnn" demonstrating approach and target tones. Once again we basically used 3rds and 7ths as target tones. At times we used other scale tones to create more interest in the line. As you play the solo listen and feel how the approach tones encourage your ear to want to hear the target tones.

Analyze this solo to discover how the note choices that make up the approach tones create the line direction and give the phrases forward motion.

by Joe Riposo

36

JOANN SOLO
#2

Bb INSTRUMENTS:
Trumpet, Cornet, Clarinet, Tenor Sax,
Soprano Sax, etc.

This is another transcribed improvised solo on the chord changes of the tune "JoAnn" demonstrating approach and target tones. Once again we basically used 3rds and 7ths as target tones. At times we used other scale tones to create more interest in the line. As you play the solo listen and feel how the approach tones encourage your ear to want to hear the target tones.

Analyze this solo to discover how the note choices that make up the approach tones create the line direction and give the phrases forward motion.

by Joe Riposo

JOANN SOLO
#2

Eb INSTRUMENTS:
Alto Sax, Baritone Sax, etc.

This is another transcribed improvised solo on the chord changes of the tune "JoAnn" demonstrating approach and target tones. Once again we basically used 3rds and 7ths as target tones. At times we used other scale tones to create more interest in the line. As you play the solo listen and feel how the approach tones encourage your ear to want to hear the target tones.

Analyze this solo to discover how the note choices that make up the approach tones create the line direction and give the phrases forward motion.

by Joe Riposo

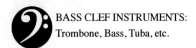

JOANN SOLO
#2

This is another transcribed improvised solo on the chord changes of the tune "JoAnn" demonstrating approach and target tones. Once again we basically used 3rds and 7ths as target tones. At times we used other scale tones to create more interest in the line. As you play the solo listen and feel how the approach tones encourage your ear to want to hear the target tones.

Analyze this solo to discover how the note choices that make up the approach tones create the line direction and give the phrases forward motion.

by Joe Riposo

CODA

Now that you have successfully learned and practiced to perfect what you have learned as described in this book I encourage you to listen with a purpose to many improvised solos played and recorded by some of the best jazz players. You should now listen to how the player approaches the target tones and creates the forward motion in his/her improvised line. Listening with a purpose to these jazz players will help you to develop your jazz vocabulary so you can improvise with ease and make musical sense.

At this point you also need to analyze written solos. Look at many published solos and analyze them to discover what kind of approach and target tones are used. Why is it that players play the same chord changes but always sound different? What makes the improvised line exciting to listen to? What is it in an improvised melodic line that makes you want to hear more? Hopefully this book has answered these questions for you, but you need to listen to improvised solos to confirm the meaningful knowledge you have obtained. Confirmation will strengthen your application of the concept described in this book.

Thanks to Jamey Aebersold you can purchase numerous transcribed solos to analyze. I suggest you bracket the approach tones and label the target tones as we did with the improvised solos of "JoAnn". This is a great learning experience you owe yourself. You should also take the time to transcribe solos from recordings. This will help to develop your ear to hear the approach and target tones. Another very important experience in the learning process is to record and transcribe your own improvised solos. I suggest you record your playing every time you perform for this purpose.

ABOUT THE AUTHOR

Joe Riposo, the Director of Jazz Studies at Syracuse University, is a saxophonist, clarinetist, composer, arranger and educator.

He's the former Director of Music Education for the Liverpool Central School District, where he worked for 31 years. Riposo served as past president of the New York State Unit of the International Association of Jazz Educators and as the IAJE's North Eastern Division Coordinator.

Riposo has served as Jazz Coordinator and Clinician for the New York State School Music Association from which he received the presidential medallion. Riposo holds the New York State School Music Association certification as a Woodwind Adjudicator and as State Jazz Adjudicator.

He remains extremely active as a performer, having worked in house bands for nationally known artists such as Tony Bennett, Sammy Davis, Jr. Nat King Cole, Ella Fitzgerald, the McGuire Sisters and many others. He played a special performance with Woody Herman's New Thundering Herd on tour with Jack E. Leonard and Tony Bennett.

Riposo has also performed in backing bands for Diane Schuur, Harry Connick Jr. and Natalie Cole. He has also conducted jazz ensembles featuring guest soloists such as Dizzy Gillespie, Phil Woods, Marvin Stamm, Glenn Drewes, Darius Brubeck, Nick Brignola and Bob Kindred.

Riposo appears frequently as clinician, adjudicator, guest conductor and soloist in jazz festivals across the U.S. He has composed several published jazz scores and is the author of the book, Jazz Improvisation "The Whole-Brain Approach" Improving Improvisation through Understanding Hemisphericity, which was recently republished in its fourth edition. His most recent publications include the LMI Recorder Method (1999) and a second recorder method book published by Increase Music (2002). As a contracted writer Joe has numerous compositions published by Increase Music and Walrus Music Publishers.

In 2008, Jamey Aebersold published Riposo's recent book, BeBop Scales: Jazz Scales And Patterns In All 12 Keys for treble and bass clef instruments (Ordering Codes: Treble = BEBOP; Bass = BEBOP-BC).

Riposo received the Outstanding Jazz Educator's Award from the National Band Association for effective leadership in instrumental music education by developing successful concert and jazz bands in America's schools.

Nov. 21, 1997, Riposo was inducted in the Syracuse Area Music Awards (Sammys) Music Hall of Fame. On June 8, 2003, he was also inducted into the Liverpool Central School District's Fine Arts Hall of Fame.

He received the 2008 Jazz Educator of the Year Award presented by the Central New York Jazz Arts Foundation. Most recently, Riposo received the Syracuse Symphony Orchestra musicians' award for Outstanding Music Educator of 2009.